Overcoming ANXIETY

Learning not to WORRY

Jasmine Brooke

FOX EYE
PUBLISHING

Bear felt **WORRIED** all the time. She felt **ANXIOUS** about many different things.

Bear **WORRIED** every day about being late for school. She **WORRIED** about forgetting her lunch.

She also WORRIED about her work. Bear was WORRIED so much of the time that it often stopped her having fun.

At school, Mrs Tree told everyone that the next day they were going on a class trip to the cinema. The class was very excited, all except ... Bear.

Bear was not excited. She was **WORRIED** because there were so very many things to be **WORRIED** about!

As poor Bear packed her lunchbox in the morning, she felt very ANXIOUS. What if she forgot to take her lunch? What if she left it on the bus?

"Are you excited, Bear?" Zebra asked as they queued for the bus. "Today will be such fun!" "No," sighed Bear. "It's such a **WORRY**."

Bear was so **WORRIED** that she couldn't **RELAX** and have fun.

As Bear sat on the bus, she felt **ANXIOUS** again. What if the bus broke down? What if the driver couldn't find his way? What if Bear missed the bus on the way home? Would she have to stay at the cinema all day? "Oh no," sighed Bear. "It's all such a **WORRY**."

Bear was so **WORRIED**, she didn't even notice she wasn't having fun.

At the cinema, Bear was worried again. How would she buy her ticket? What if she lost it?

Perhaps she'd forgotten her money and wouldn't be able to buy a ticket at all!
"Oh no," sighed Bear.
"It's all such a **WORRY**."

Bear was so **WORRIED** that she couldn't stop thinking everything was going to **GO WRONG**.

When Bear sat in her seat, she felt ANXIOUS again. She wanted to eat her lunch and her popcorn too. Just like everyone else. But what if she made a noise or a mess?

"Oh no," sighed Bear. "It's all such a WORRY."

All through the **WORRYING**, Mrs Tree had been watching. She could see how **ANXIOUS** Bear was. Mrs Tree said, "Come sit with me, Bear. There's really no need to **FRET**."

Then, Mrs Tree took a bite of her lunch and smiled, "Everything will work out OK."

So Bear ate her popcorn
and lunch. She made a mess
but it was OK.

15

After the film, Bear caught the bus. She kept hold of her lunchbox, and the driver didn't get lost. Everything was OK.

"Did you have fun, Bear?" Zebra asked as the bus arrived home. "Oh yes," said Bear. "Everything worked out Ok. I wasn't **WORRIED** at all!"

Bear had learnt how to manage her **WORRYING**. She had learnt not to be so **ANXIOUS**. Most importantly, Bear had learnt to have **FUN**!

Words and feelings

Bear felt very worried in this story. She felt very anxious too.

WORRY

FRET

There are a lot of words to do with feeling worried and anxious in this book. Can you remember all of them?

ANXIOUS

RELAX

WORRIED

How to discuss the story

When you have finished reading the story, use these questions and discussion points to examine the theme of the story with children and explore the emotions and behaviours within it:

- What do you think the story was about? Have you been in a situation in which you were worried? What was that situation? For example, did you go on a school trip that made you feel anxious? Encourage the children to talk about their experiences.
- Talk about ways that people can cope with anxiety. For example, think about how you can tell yourself that everything will work out OK, just as it did for Bear in the story. Talk to the children about what tools they think might work for them and why.
- Discuss what it is like to manage worrying. Explain that Bear worried about everything, and that stopped her enjoying herself.
- Talk about why it is important to manage anxiety so that it does not escalate out of control, and that by managing worries people can learn to try new things and enjoy new experiences.

How to read the story

Before beginning the story, ensure that the children you are reading to are relaxed and focused.

Take time to look at the enlarged words and the illustrations, and discuss what this book might be about before reading the story.

New words can be tricky for young children to approach. Sounding them out first, slowly and repeatedly, can help children to learn the words and become familiar with them.

How to discuss the story

When you have finished reading the story, use these questions and discussion points to examine the theme of the story with children and explore the emotions and behaviours within it:

- What do you think the story was about? Have you been in a situation in which you were worried? What was that situation? For example, did you go on a school trip that made you feel anxious? Encourage the children to talk about their experiences.
- Talk about ways that people can cope with anxiety. For example, think about how you can tell yourself that everything will work out OK, just as it did for Bear in the story. Talk to the children about what tools they think might work for them and why.
- Discuss what it is like to manage worrying. Explain that Bear worried about everything, and that stopped her enjoying herself.
- Talk about why it is important to manage anxiety so that it does not escalate out of control, and that by managing worries people can learn to try new things and enjoy new experiences.

Titles in the series

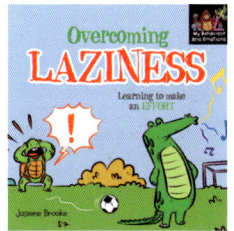 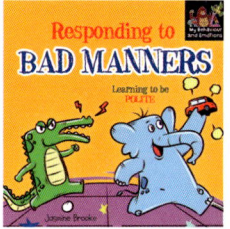 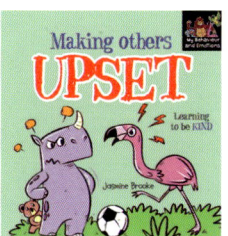 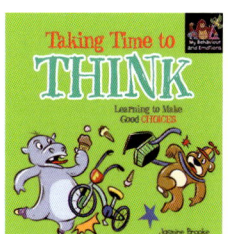 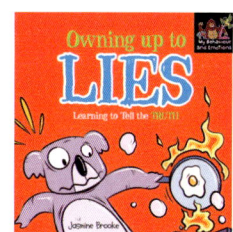
 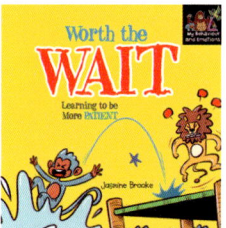 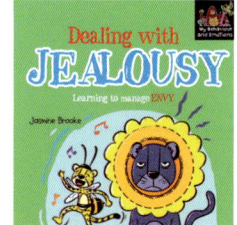  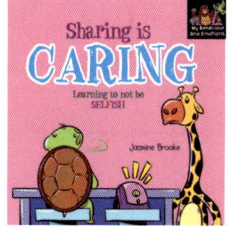
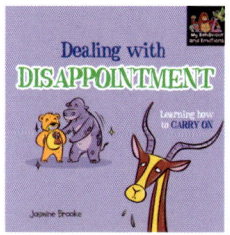  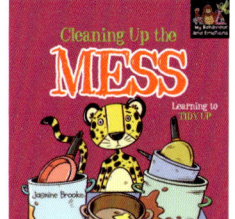 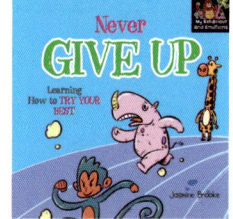 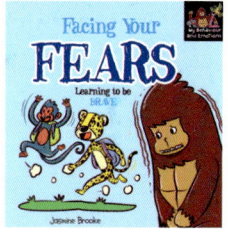
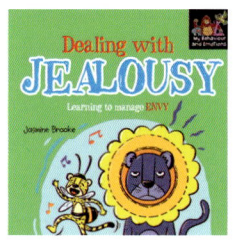  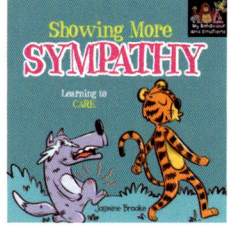 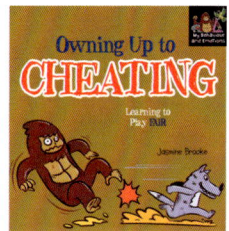 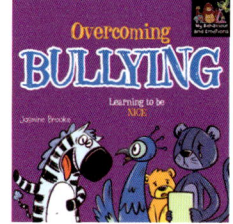

First published in 2023 by Fox Eye Publishing
Unit 31, Vulcan House Business Centre,
Vulcan Road, Leicester, LE5 3EF
www.foxeyepublishing.com

Copyright © 2023 Fox Eye Publishing
All rights reserved. No portion of this book may be reproduced in any form without permission from the publisher, except as permitted by U.K. copyright law.

Author: Jasmine Brooke
Art director: Paul Phillips
Cover designer: Emma Bailey & Salma Thadha
Editor: Jenny Rush

All illustrations by Novel

ISBN 978-1-80445-298-1

A catalogue record for this book is available from the British Library

Printed in China